To arms for]

A pageant of the war for schoe

Catherine T. Bryce

Alpha Editions

This edition published in 2023

ISBN : 9789362090218

Design and Setting By
Alpha Editions
www.alphaedis.com
Email - info@alphaedis.com

Contents

CHARACTERS

BELGIUM	BRITAIN	FRANCE	ITALY	
(*Britain's Daughters*)				
	ENGLAND	IRELAND	SCOTLAND	WALES
	CANADA	INDIA	AUSTRALIA	NEW ZEALAND
SERBIA	MONTENEGRO	PORTUGAL	SAN MARINO	
ROUMANIA	GREECE	RUSSIA	POLAND	JAPAN

AMERICA

AMERICAN SOLDIERS, SAILORS, Y. M. C. A., and RED CROSS MEN

NOTE

All the allies who entered the war previous to America's entry are mentioned, but not in chronological order. That order is as follows:—

- Serbia, July 28, 1914

- Russia, Aug. 1, 1914

- France, Aug. 3, 1914

- Belgium, Aug. 4, 1914

- Britain, Aug. 4, 1914

- Montenegro, Aug. 8, 1914

- Japan, Aug. 23, 1914

- Italy, May 24, 1915

- San Marino, May 24, 1915

- Portugal, Mar. 9, 1916

- Roumania, Aug. 27, 1916

- Greece, Nov. 28, 1918

- United States, Apr. 6, 1917

TO ARMS FOR LIBERTY

NO. 1. INTRODUCTORY MUSIC: suggesting strife, discord—War.

THE CURTAIN RISES. BELGIUM, *a girl dressed in Belgian costume, clutching Belgium's flag to her heart, enters and rushes to center of stage.*

BELGIUM:

Hark! Hark! Do you not hear it? The heavy measured tread, the rumbling cannon, the screaming shot, the bursting shell, the anguished cries of my brave children?

Look! Look! Can you not see? Nay, thank God you cannot see what I have been forced to look upon. (BELGIUM *covers her eyes.*) Oh, my sons! My brave sons—for ye were brave! Ye fell, but ye fell with your faces to the foe, defending your homes, your country, and your honor! Still ye are gone and I am left desolate.

Oh, my children, my children! None too young, none too old, none too brave, none too tender to escape the brutal destroyer! All lost, lost, lost!

(*The distant strains of "Sambre et Meuse" are heard and* FRANCE, *a girl dressed in classic white robe, wearing liberty cap, and carrying tricolor, enters. She goes to* BELGIUM'S *side and places her hand on the latter's shoulder.*)

FRANCE:

Arise, my Sister. All is *not* lost! Thine honor and thy truth and thy loyalty are all untarnished. Pure and white they shine before the eyes of all the world. Till the stars fade and the sun dies, all men shall say of thee, "Belgium's is a consecrated,—Belgium's is a holy ground!"

Lift up thy flag. It has never trailed in the dust, and it never shall. Together, shoulder to shoulder, we will face the foe, and *They Shall Not Pass.* On, on my Sister, on to Victory!

NO. 2. *CHORUS*: "THE MARSEILLAISE":

Ye sons of Freedom, wake to glory!

Hark! Hark! what myriads bid you rise!

Your children, wives, and grandsires hoary,

Behold their tears and hear their cries!

Shall hateful tyrants, mischief breeding,

With hireling hosts, a ruffian band,
Affright and desolate the land,
While peace and liberty lie bleeding?

To arms! To arms! ye brave!
The avenging sword unsheathe;
March on! March on! all hearts resolved
On victory or death.

Now, now the dangerous storm is rolling,
Which treacherous kings, confederate, raise;
The dogs of war, let loose, are howling,
And lo! our fields and cities blaze;
And shall we basely view the ruin,
While lawless force with guilty stride,
Spreads desolation far and wide,
With crimes and blood his hands imbruing?

O Liberty! can man resign thee,
Once having felt thy generous flame?
Can dungeons, bolts, or bars confine thee?
Or whips thy noble spirit tame?
Too long the world has wept bewailing
That falsehood's dagger tyrants wield,
But freedom is our sword and shield,
And all their arts are unavailing.

(*While the chorus sing "The Marseillaise,"* France *and* Belgium *stand with unfurled flags.* France, *several steps in front of* Belgium, *appears to lead the music. Appropriate pantomime during the singing will help.* Belgium, *too, shows the effects of the music, first, by an awakened look, then by advancing one step at a time, until she is shoulder to shoulder with* France *when the song ends.*)

BELGIUM:

Dare I, dare I believe?

FRANCE:

Believe? Believe the victory will be ours? Aye, never doubt it. Nor shall we fight alone. Britain joins our cause.

BELGIUM:

Britain? Britain, the proud, the arrogant! Why think ye she will come?

FRANCE:

Because she hath promised.

BELGIUM:

Promised! Promised! Methinks I have heard that the promises of strong nations are but "scraps of paper."

FRANCE:

But not Britain's promises! Proud, arrogant, and strong she may be, but when was she known to break a treaty? She hath promised her fleets to guard my shore and I rely on her word. Britain never shall be foresworn.

(*MUSIC: "Rule Britannia" heard as at a distance.*)

BELGIUM:

Hark! What is that?

FRANCE:

There! it is she! Did I not tell you Britain would keep her word?

NO. 3. *CHORUS*: "RULE BRITANNIA":

When Britain first at Heaven's command,

Arose from out the azure main,

This was the charter of the land,

And guardian angels sang the strain:

Rule, Britannia, rule the waves,

Britons never shall be slaves.

Still more majestic shalt thou rise,

More dreadful from each foreign stroke;

As the loud blast that tears the skies

Serves but to root thy native oak.

Rule, Britannia, rule the waves,

Britons never shall be slaves.

Thee, haughty tyrants ne'er shall tame;

All their attempts to bear thee down

Will but arouse thy generous flame,

But work their woe, and thy renown.

Rule Britannia, rule the waves,

Britons never shall be slaves.

(As the chorus reach the refrain "Rule Britannia, rule the waves!" Britain enters. She is dressed as Britannia. Accompanying her are, England, clad in white and rose pink, bearing the English standard; Scotland, clad in white and purple, bearing the Scottish standard; Ireland, dressed in white and green, bearing Irish flag; Wales dressed in white, bearing the Welsh flag; Canada, dressed in white robe, trimmed with maple leaves, bearing Canadian flag, Australia and New Zealand, dressed in robes similar to Britain's other daughters, India, clad in native costume. Britain with her companions grouped about her, occupies the center of the stage, Belgium and France, the front-left and right.)

BRITAIN *(touching the Union Jack on her shield with her trident, then extending it to* FRANCE):

I have come, my Sister.

FRANCE *(impulsively rushing forward and clasping* BRITAIN'S *hand)*:

I said ye would come. *(Turning to* BELGIUM.*)* Said I not so?

BELGIUM:

I had thought—I feared—

BRITAIN *(stretching her hand to* BELGIUM):

I understand, say no more.

"Men whispered that our arm was weak,

Men said our blood was cold,

And that our hearts no longer speak

The clarion-note of old;

But let the spear and sword draw near

The sleeping lion's den,

His island shore shall start once more

To life with armèd men."

BRITAIN (continuing):

Nor think, O Belgium, that thy bravery and thy chivalry count for naught.

"Whatever men have done, man may,—

The deeds you wrought are not in vain!"

(To FRANCE): Not only do I guard the ocean with my fleets; I bring here my children to aid you in upholding justice, truth and liberty.

England, what is thy message?

ENGLAND (saluting):

Ready!

"Old England's sons are English yet,

Old England's hearts are strong;

And still she wears her coronet

Aflame with sword and song.

As in their pride our fathers died,

If need be, so die we;

So wield we still, gainsay who will,

The sceptre of the sea."

BRITAIN:

"England, stand fast; let heart and hand be steady; Be thy first word thy last,—Ready, aye, ready!"

NO. 4. *CHORUS*: "YE MARINERS OF ENGLAND!"

The meteor flag of England
Shall yet terrific burn;
Till danger's troubled night depart
And the star of peace return.
Then, then, ye ocean-warriors!
Our song and feast shall flow
To the fame of your name,
When the storm has ceased to blow!
When the fiery fight is heard no more,
And the storm has ceased to blow!

BRITAIN:
Ireland, what message do you bring?
IRELAND (*stepping forward and saluting*):

And when did Erin e'er hold back,
When Freedom called for men?
I'm with you to the finish, friends,
For God and the Right, Amen!

ALL (*with upraised banners*):
"God and the Right, Amen!"

NO. 5. *CHORUS*: "THE MINSTREL-BOY":

The minstrel-boy to the war is gone,
In the ranks of death you'll find him;
His father's sword he has girded on,
And his wild harp slung behind him.
"Land of song!" cried the warrior-bard,
"Though all the world betrays thee,
One sword, at least, thy rights shall guard,

One faithful heart shall praise thee."

BRITAIN:

Scotland, what is thy message?

SCOTLAND (*stepping forward and saluting*):

From Scotia's Isles and storm-tossed shore,
From fortress-rock and peaceful glen,
Come ranks of lion-hearted men—
Come clansmen true as knights of old,
Meet warriors for achievement bold,
Loving their home, but Freedom more!

(*Continues, peering and pointing as if seeing a far-off vision*):

I see their plaids and tartans wave,
I know them, bravest of the brave!
I see their eyes with purpose fired;
I know their hearts with right inspired;
I know their purpose—all mine own—
That Freedom shall resume her throne!
Hear! hear their slogan stern and old—
Meet slogan for my warriors bold!

NO. 6 *CHORUS*: "SCOTS WHA HAE":

Wha for Scotland's king and law
Freedom's sword will strongly draw,
Freeman stand, or freeman fa',
Let him follow me!

By oppression's woes and pains!
By your sons in servile chains,

- 8 -

We will drain our dearest veins,

But they shall be free!

Lay the proud usurpers low!

Tyrants fall in every foe!

Liberty at every blow!

Let us do or die!

ALL:

"Let us do or die!"

BRITAIN:

Wales, what is thy message?

WALES (*stepping forward and saluting*):

Since Arthur formed his table round,

Within my favored land,

And taught each page, and squire, and knight,

For Freedom's cause to stand,

And 'gainst oppression urge their might,

My sons have stood for God and right.

And so we join you in this fight!

NO. 7. *CHORUS*: "HARLECH":

Men of Harlech! in the hollow,

Do you hear like rushing billow,

Wave on wave that surging follow,

Battle's distant sound?

'Tis the tramp of Saxon foeman,

Saxon spearmen, Saxon bowmen,

Be they knights, or hinds, or yeomen,

They shall bite the ground!

Loose the folds asunder,

Flag we conquer under!

The placid sky now bright on high,

Shall launch its bolts in thunder,

Onward! 'tis our country needs us.

He is bravest, he who leads us!

Honor's self now proudly heads us!

Freedom, God, and Right!

BRITAIN:

Canada, youngest of my daughters, ye send each gallant son forth, a maiden-knight, to earn his spurs. What is thy message?

CANADA (advancing and saluting):

"I give my soldier boy a blade,

In fair Damascus fashioned well;

Who first the glittering falchion swayed,

Who first beneath its fury fell,

I know not; but I hope to know,

That for no mean or hireling trade,

To guard no feeling base or low—

I give my soldier boy the blade!

"For country's claim at honor's call,

For outraged friend, insulted maid.

At mercy's voice to bid it fall—

I give my soldier boy the blade!"

FRANCE:

The sword unsheathed in such a cause will ne'er be tarnished. It will return to you, my Sister, laureled with the deeds of thy brave sons. I know it! I know it!

NO. 8. *CHORUS*: "THE MAPLE LEAF FOREVER!"

On many a hard-fought battle field

Our brave fathers, side by side,

For loved ones, home and freedom dear,

Firmly stood and nobly died.

And those dear rights which they maintained

We swear to yield them never;

God save our land and Heaven bless

The Maple Leaf forever.

The Maple Leaf, our emblem dear,

May we forsake it never;

God save our land and Heaven bless

The Maple Leaf forever!

BRITAIN:

India, what message do you bear?

INDIA (*advancing and making native salaam*):

I bring thee the loving homage,

Of a people thy justice has won,

I pledge ye our faith and our service.

Till the day of the despot is done.

BRITAIN:

Well spoken, my daughter. I knew I could rely on thy loyalty. Australia, fair and independent, what word do you bring?

AUSTRALIA (*advancing and saluting*):

My great grey ships are on their way,

Plowing the crested wave,

A precious freight they're carrying

My gallant sons and brave.

BRITAIN:

Aye, gallant and brave and strong are they! New Zealand, what is thy message?

NEW ZEALAND (advancing and saluting):

I heard you calling, Mother,

I bring you of my best,

My splendid men, my Mother,

God guard them in this test.

BRITAIN AND HER DAUGHTERS (with upraised faces):

God, guard our men!

NO. 9. *CHORUS*: (*Tune*—"GOD SAVE THE KING"):

"God bless our splendid men,

Send them safe home again,

God bless our men.

Keep them victorious,

Strong, clean and glorious,

They are so dear to us,

God bless our men."

(*During the singing of the above verse, all stand in an attitude of supplication.*)

BELGIUM:

O Britain, well mayest thou be proud! With such loyal daughters and such gallant sons, thou art invincible.

FRANCE:

Lo! one crowned with sorrow approaches. It is Serbia and with her comes her neighbor, Montenegro. (*Enter* SERBIA *and* MONTENEGRO. *Each is dressed in National costume and carries National flag.*)

NO. 10. *CHORUS*: "SERBIAN HYMN":

Up and arise the Nations call you!

Men of Serbia rise as one,

Honor calls, whate'er befall you,

Up and strike till Freedom's won!

Though the wrong may seem to conquer,

Truth and Justice will prevail,

Up and onward to the battle,

Freedom's cause shall never fail.

Up and strike till Freedom's won!

Strike till Freedom's won!

SERBIA (*holding forth her hands as begging for sympathy*):

Woe, woe is me, that the deed of one of my weakest sons should be made the excuse for this world-wide war! Mad was the deed, and mad the boy— but must the world be set on fire for such a cause?

I would have prevented it if I could. Did I not yield all, all, all I could and save mine honor? Speak to me! Tell me, my Sisters, that I am guiltless of this world-agony!

ALL (*stepping forward and extending the right hand to Serbia*):

We pronounce thee guiltless.

(*The last strains of the Russian Hymn are heard and* Russia *enters, followed by* Poland. Russia *is clad in National costume and carries the Russian flag.* Poland *is in characteristic costume, but carries no flag.*)

BELGIUM:

O Russia, dost thou too love Freedom?

RUSSIA:

I've dreamed a dream—a wondrous dream—

I've dreamed it long—aye, long;

And in my dream, my people stand—

Brave *freemen*, true and strong.

No men have longed for Liberty

As Russia's sons have yearned,

In the hearts that know oppression,

Freedom's light most fiercely burns.

The day will come—I know not when

But still mine eyes shall see

My dream—my dream of dreams—come true,

And Russia's sons be free.

NO. 11. *CHORUS*: HYMN TO NEW RUSSIA:

New Russia, rise and proudly stand

Where men and heroes are;

Go forth with Freedom, hand in hand,

Thine eyes upon a star!

Create a land where men are peers,

Where laws, not monarchs, reign,

And take thine heritage of years

Made sacred by thy pain!

ALL:

May Russia's sons be free!

FRANCE:

And Poland's, too. Brave men whose hearts have ever yearned for Freedom's crown!

NO. 12. *CHORUS*: POLAND FAIR:

Poland Fair, thou bright and lovely land,

Ne'er to be forsaken;

Loyal sons obey thy proud command:

Ev'ry soul awaken!

Sacred land, we love thee well,

Our hearts unite beneath thy spell;

Take, O Country, all thy sons can give,

Poland fair, thy name shall live!

(*A trumpet call sounds.*)

FRANCE:

Hark! Another friend approaches from the fair South!

NO. 13. *CHORUS:* GARIBALDI'S HYMN:

All forward to battle! the trumpets are crying,

All forward! all forward! our old flag is flying.

When liberty calls us, we linger no longer.

Ye tyrants, come on! Tho' a thousand to one!

Hurrah for the banner, the flag of the free!

(*Enter* ITALY, *dressed in National costume.*)

FRANCE:

Now, welcome, Sister Italy. I have looked for thy coming.

BELGIUM:

Twice welcome art thou, for I, too, hoped for your aid.

BRITAIN:

Thrice welcome art thou. For well I know that in thee still lives the greatness that was Rome.

ITALY:

Yea, and dauntless as Romans of old come my sons to strike for liberty. Now as then—

The horsemen and the footmen

Are pouring in amain

From many a stately market place,

From many a fruitful plain,

From many a lonely hamlet,

Which, hid by beech and pine,

Like an eagle's nest, hangs on the crest

Of purple Apennine.

And the same spirit that urged the hero of old to face the foe, fires the hearts
and strengthens the hand of my younger sons, for—

"How can a man die better

Than facing fearful odds,

For the ashes of his fathers,

And the temples of his Gods?"

NO. 14. *CHORUS*: "SOUND! TRUMPET!"

Hark! from the vine-cover'd valley,

Up to the mountains above,

Loud rings the signal to rally

Under the banner we love.

Aloft bright pennons are glancing,

And ev'ry heart beats high;

Proudly the hosts are advancing

To fight and if need be, to die!

Chorus.

Sound! trumpet, sound! let the battle-cry

Re-echo from mountain to strand!

Sound ye the strain that shall lead us on

To strike for Italia, our land!

God of the fathers who perish'd

Seeking the birthright we claim,

Thine is the flow'r we have cherished,

Ne'er let it wither in shame!

The fires of Freedom are lighted,

With deathless flame they glow;

Forward! in faith all united,

To strike and to vanquish the foe!

BELGIUM:

O Italy, thy proud spirit shall again triumph!

(*Music—Japanese National Song—is heard off stage.*)

NO. 15. *CHORUS*: JAPANESE NATIONAL SONG:

"Just as leaves by autumn sown

Red and fair to earth are blown,

Just as these never cease

Year by year to shed their peace,

Thus shall be Freedom's reign to Eternity."

(*As Chorus sings the last lines* Japan *enters. She is clad in Japanese costume and carries the Japanese flag. During the singing of the last line, she makes the National salaam, remaining with her forehead to the ground until the last note has died away.*)

BRITAIN:

We bid you welcome, my Sister. Great indeed is the cause that unites East and West.

FRANCE:

Freedom's cause alone can work so great a miracle.

JAPAN:

To Eastward ringing, to Eastward winging,

Came Freedom's call to me.

"Send forth thy sons, thy gallant sons,

To guard fair Liberty!"

To Westward winging, to Westward bringing

My dauntless sons so true,

I've travelled half way round the earth

To take my stand with you.

(*Martial airs heard off stage.*)

MONTENEGRO:

Hark! Others come to join us from the South.

(*Enter* SAN MARINO, PORTUGAL, ROUMANIA, *and* GREECE. *Each is dressed in National costume and carries National flag.*)

SAN MARINO:

As the oldest, though the smallest, Republic in the world I have come to strike a blow for Freedom.

PORTUGAL:

And I will stand by you, my Sister, till

"Freedom's perils be outbraved,

And Freedom's flag, wherever waved,

Shall overshadow none enslaved."

NO. 16. *CHORUS*: OH, COME, ALL YE VALIANT:

(*Tune—Portuguese Hymn*):

Oh, come all ye valiant,

Join our high endeavor,

Oh, come ye, oh, come ye, now in

Freedom's name.

Oh, come, strike for Freedom

Our country now is calling,

Oh, come and strike for Freedom!

Oh, come and strike for Freedom!

Oh, come and strike for Freedom!

Our God, and Right!

ROUMANIA:

"We are they whose firm battalions
Trained to fight, not fly,
Know the cause of good will triumph,
It will triumph though we die!"

NO. 17. *CHORUS*: ROUMANIAN HYMN:

Long live fair Liberty,
Honor and Peace she brings—
Peace to our well-loved land,
Honor to mankind.
Freedom all glorious in God's own gift to all,
We will fight; we may die,
But right shall ever stand.
O God Almighty, O God of Heaven,
Uphold with mighty hand,
Fair Freedom's name and cause!

O may the day soon come
When peace on earth is won
All strife and hate be past.
Truth and right defended
Right shall reign glorious—all men shall hear its call.
Truth shall rise; Right prevail
And peace at last shall come.
O God Almighty, O heav'nly Father,
Uphold with mighty hand,
Fair Freedom's name and cause!

GREECE:

Doubt not that my sons will acquit themselves as did their fathers "on old Plataea's day." They are

"True as the steel of their tried blades,

Heroes in heart and hand,

The sons of sires who conquered there,

With arm to strike and soul to dare,

As quick, as far as they."

BRITAIN:

Ah, my Sister, may ye prove to the world that "the glory that was Greece" still abides with thy sons.

FRANCE:

Still others come to join us. From the frozen North, from the sunny South, and from the far East they come.

BELGIUM:

What of the West? What of America—the great, the strong, the free—is she coming?

FRANCE:

Not yet.

BRITAIN:

But she will come! Well I know her. Ours are

"Sons of the self-same race.

And blood of the self-same clan."

ITALY:

Yes, she will come. Well is she named Columbia, after my gallant son Columbus. Can'st see him as he steered his bark to Columbia's shore, when

"Pale and worn, he kept his deck,

And peered through darkness. Ah, that night

Of all dark nights! And then a speck—

A light! A light! A light! A light!

It grew—a starlit flag unfurled,

It grew to be Time's burst of dawn.

He gained a world; he gave that world

Its grandest lesson: 'On and On.'"

That light became the light of Freedom. That light is still upheld clear and pure by Columbia. In that light she will press "on and on" till tyranny be banished from the earth.

FRANCE:

Aye, she will come, if but to pay back the debt of gratitude she owes us for our aid when she won her Independence.

BELGIUM:

She must come, for we need her aid.

BRITAIN:

America is proud; she will repay her debt of gratitude, France. America is generous; she will send you aid, Belgium.

NO. 18. Music of Largo. (*All look to the rear. Enter*—Charity, Hope, *and* Faith; Charity *carries large cornucopia*.)

CHARITY:

We bear ye greetings and gifts from America.

BELGIUM:

Ah, I know you. Ye are Charity.

CHARITY:

Call me by my new name, Love, for the love of America sends me and my Sisters with help and messages of cheer.

HOPE:

I am Hope. Never despair. Ye shall triumph. "Be staunch, and valiant, and free, and strong."

FAITH:

I am Faith. Press on—

"I do not know beneath what sky

Nor on what seas shall be thy fate;

I only know it shall be high,

I only know it shall be great."

(*Enter* Mercy, *a Red Cross nurse,* Charity *takes her by the hand and leads her forward.*)

MERCY:

Thy Sister, America, has heard thy call for help, and sends me. I am ready for service.

NO. 19. *CHORUS*: THE RED CROSS:

(*Tune—Battle Hymn of the Republic*):

Mine eyes have seen the glory of the Red Cross on the White;

It carries ease and comfort to the soldiers in the fight,

It strengthens their endeavors in the battle for the right,

Its mercy never fails!

Hail the Red Cross then forever,

Its mercy never fails!

At the call of suffering thousands it now flies across the sea,

The homeless hosts of Belgium know its mercy kind and free,

In prison camps in Europe it breathes hope and liberty,

Its mercy never fails!

Hail the Red Cross then forever,

Its mercy never fails!

FRANCE:

Your gifts and messages bring comfort and inspiration, but why does America wait?

CHARITY:

"With malice toward none, with charity for all," America has sought to live at peace with all men. "With firmness in the right as God gives her to see the right," she will act when the time comes.

BRITAIN (to FRANCE *and* BELGIUM):

Said I not so? (*Turning toward West with outstretched arms*):

"Columbia, Sister of the West,

With all of Nature's gifts endowed,

With all of Heaven's mercies blessed,

Nor of thy power unduly proud,

Peerless in courage, force, and skill,

And godlike in thy strength of will,—

"Before thy feet the ways divide;

One path leads up to heights sublime;

Downward the other slopes, where bide

The refuse and the wreck of Time.

Choose, then, nor falter at the start,

O choose the nobler path and part!"

FRANCE (stepping to BRITAIN'S *side, continues*):

"Be thou the guardian of the weak,

Of the unfriended, thou the friend;

No guerdon for thy valor seek.

No end beyond the avowèd end.

Wouldst thou thy godlike power preserve,

Be godlike in the will to serve."

(*Others join* Britain *and* France *in silent supplication. Music softly, first lines of "Star-Spangled Banner." While music sounds, the American Flag is unfurled from above over stage. Immediately* America *enters. She is dressed like* Columbia *and carries a lighted torch. While she stands a moment in the center at the rear, music changes to "Hail Columbia," while all on stage salute her.*)

- 23 -

ALL:

Hail! Hail! Columbia!

AMERICA:

"Prince of Light, or Prince of Darkness!
I have chosen for the world,
On the side of deathless freedom
I my banner have unfurled."

AMERICA (to Belgium):

"Little Belgium, crushed and bleeding,
Martyred by the cruel horde,
Crowned with thorns, yet bravely fighting,
Thou shalt live to be restored!"

(to France):

"France, the fair, with face uplifted,
Radiant courage on you waits,
Thou shalt beat the hordes of Prussia,
Seeking entrance at thy gates."

FRANCE:

They shall not pass! They shall not pass!

AMERICA (to Britain):

"Britons, ye
Who guard the sacred outpost, not in vain
Hold your proud peril! Freemen undefiled
Keep watch and ward! Let battlements be piled
Around your cliffs; fleets marshalled, till the main
Sink under them; and if your courage wane,

Through force or fraud, look westward to your child."

BRITAIN:

"Now fling them out to the breeze,
Shamrock, Thistle and Rose,
And the Star-Spangled Banner unfurl with these—
A message to friends and to foes
Wherever the sails of peace are seen, and wherever
The war wind blows—

"A message to bond and thrall to wake,
For whenever we come, we twain,
The throne of the tyrant shall rock and quake,
And his menace be void and vain,
For you are lords of a strong land,
And we are lords of the main."

(*While* Britain *speaks,* Ireland, Scotland, *and* England *group flags beside Stars and Stripes.*)

AMERICA (*to Canada*):

"Valiant neighbor of my home land,
The flower of thy Canadian youth;
At the front where danger gathers
Bravely stand for God and Truth."

(*to Italy*):

"In the bright and sunny Southland,
Where thy sons are fighting sore,
Garibaldi's spirit liveth
As the wine of life they pour."

(to All):

"Noble Sisterhood of Nations,

I have joined thy vanguard, too;

Freedom's torch is brightly burning,

And I pass it on to you."

(Waves torch and all light electric torches which have been concealed; these they raise aloft as America *continues)*:

"Bear aloft its sacred message

To all nations of the earth,

Till a world-wide peace forever

Comes to bless us with new birth."

NO. 20. *CHORUS*: HAIL, COLUMBIA:

Firm, united let us be,

Rallying around our Liberty,

As a band of brothers joined,

Peace and safety we shall find.

(Bugles heard off stage.)

AMERICA:

They come! my gallant sons! All are with me. *(Unfurls service flag.)* See my service flag—a star for every state and none missing.

NO. 21. MEDLEY OF PATRIOTIC AIRS.

(American Soldiers and Sailors *march in; a line of* Red Cross Men *in the van. When all are in places at the rear of the stage their leader approaches and salutes* Columbia. *She hands him the service flag which he passes to a soldier who holds it at the right of the large American flag. A* Red Cross Man *holds the flag of the Red Cross at the left.* Columbia *and the leader of the soldiers stand before the large flag.)*

LEADER: THE AMERICAN FLAG:

Stars of the early dawning, set in a field of blue;

Stripes of the sunrise splendor, crimson and white of hue;

Flag of our fathers' fathers, born on the field of strife,

Phoenix of fiery battle, risen from human life;

Given for God and Freedom, sacred, indeed the trust

Left by the countless thousands returned to the silent dust.

Flag of a mighty nation waving aloft unfurled;

Kissed by the sun of heaven, caressed by the winds of the world.

Greater than kingly power, greater than all mankind;

Conceived in the need of the hour, inspired by the Master Mind;

Over the living children, over the laureled grave,

Streaming on high in the cloudless sky, banner our fathers gave.

Under thy spangled folds thy children await to give

All that they have or are that the flag they love shall live.

NO. 22. *CHORUS*: UNDER THE STARS AND STRIPES:

High on the world did our fathers of old,

Under the stars and stripes,

Blazon the name that we now must uphold,

Under the stars and stripes.

Vast in the past they have builded an arch

Over which Freedom has lighted her torch.

Follow it! Follow it! Come, let us march

Under the stars and stripes!

Chorus.

Under the stars and stripes,

Under the stars and stripes!

Follow it, follow it, come, let us march

Under the stars and stripes!

Follow it, follow it, come, let us march

Under the stars and stripes!

We in whose bodies the blood of them runs,

Under the stars and stripes,

We will acquit us as sons of their sons,

Under the stars and stripes.

Ever for justice, our heel upon wrong,

We in the light of our vengeance thrice strong

Rally together! Come tramping along

Under the stars and stripes!

SOLDIERS AND SAILORS (*with hands at salute*):

"I pledge allegiance to my Flag, and to the Republic for which it stands—one Nation, indivisible, with Liberty and Justice for all."

AMERICA:

"Freedom for all, forever!"

FINALE: (*Last stanza of*—STAR-SPANGLED BANNER):

CHORUS: *ALL*:

"Oh! thus be it ever, when freemen shall stand

Between their loved homes and the war's desolation,

Blessed with victory and peace, may the heaven rescued land

Praise the power that has made and preserved us a nation.

Then conquer we must, for our cause it is just,

And this be our motto: 'In God is our trust,'

And the Star-Spangled Banner in triumph shall wave

O'er the land of the free and the home of the brave!"

CURTAIN

The quotations used have been selected from the following:

READY, AYE, READY	*Herman C. Merivale*
I GIVE MY SOLDIER BOY A BLADE	*William Maginn*
HORATIUS AT THE BRIDGE	*Thomas B. Macaulay*
COLUMBUS	*Joaquin Miller*
UNMANIFEST DESTINY	*Henry Holcomb Bennett*
THE PARTING OF THE WAYS	*Joseph B. Gilder*

(To fit the context the first line of this poem has been slightly changed. The original reads, "Untrammelled Giant of the West.")

A SONG OF THE ALLIES	*Irene Brush*
TO ENGLAND	*George Henry Boker*
TO AMERICA	*Alfred Austin*
THE AMERICAN FLAG	*Charles G. Crellin*
ARMAGEDDON	*Edwin Arnold*
MARCO BOZZARIUS	*Fitz-Greene Halleck*

NOTES ON MUSIC

To fit the context the last line of the Japanese National Song has been slightly altered.

Milton Keynes UK
Ingram Content Group UK Ltd.
UKHW011125180424
441376UK00004B/224